IF YOUR NAME'S NOT

----------------------------------,

GET YOUR HANDS OFF ME!

NexGen® is an imprint of
Cook Communications Ministries, Colorado Springs, CO 80918
Cook Communications, Paris, Ontario
Kingsway Communications, Eastbourne, England

OVER THE EDGE: ULTIMATE SUBMISSION
© Copyright 2006 by Ron Luce
Ron Luce is the founder and president of Teen Mania Ministries.

The Word at Work Around the World
A vital part of Cook Communications Ministries is our international outreach, Cook Communications International (CCMI). Your purchase of this book, and of other books and Christian-growth products from Cook, enables CCMI to provide Bibles and Christian literature to people in more than 150 languages in 65 countries.

First printing 2006
Printed in China
1 2 3 4 5 6 7 8 9 10 Printing/Year 11 10 09 08 07 06

Cover Design: BMB Design
Interior Design: Helen Harrison (Ya-Ye Design)

ISBN: 0-78144-416-0

TABLE OF CONTENTS

DIG IN: THE DEVOTED WARRIOR WAS CHOCK FULL of awesome material to feed your faith—whether you gobbled it up in one weekend retreat or took it week by week in spoonfuls.

The point of this journal is to take some of the things you learned and, not only add another layer, but make it yours. Your journey with God is between the two of you. God wants to get closer to you, but He will never force His way in; only you can invite Him to take you deeper.

So make the choice to jump headlong into the water—a streamlined dive, a cannonball, a belly flop—it doesn't matter! All that matters is that you jump. Take that leap with *Over the Edge: Ultimate Submission.*

DIG IN: REVISITED

Before you dive *Over the Edge,* let's do a quick review of the *Dig In* experience.

SESSION 1: DEVOTED TO THE KING

You learned that God's kingdom is a monarchy. You also learned that "Lord" is not just something that should roll off your tongue without thinking about it; it means "master" and "owner." You pledged to be a warrior for Him since He did battle for you on the cross.

SESSION 2: TRUE POWER, TOTAL AUTHORITY

You talked about mottos, and you discussed how our Christian motto is the greatest commandment that Jesus gave us. You used props like clay to show how God can mold you when you're willing, and other props, like dog leashes and video controllers, to illustrate that God doesn't force you to obey. It's your choice.

SESSION 3: I'M YOURS FOREVER!

During this session, you really handed yourself over to God. You took a long, painful look at the crucifixion and how it should spark love and devotion from you.

SESSION 4: DEFYING THE ENEMY

You learned that you have a defined enemy, Satan, and that he is at work trying to trip you up. You also saw that there is no neutral territory: you choose God and His ways or you choose Satan and his ways. You also spent time talking about the world and its values, and then you symbolically turned your back on the list your group had made of those worldly values.

SESSION FIVE: HIS AGENTS

In this session you learned that God doesn't want you to be an undercover Christian. He gave you a light so that others could see its brightness. You talked about how even though this world is not where our true citizenship is, you are here for a purpose: to point others to Christ.

SESSION SIX: COURAGE UNDER FIRE

You heard stories of courage, dramatic and plain, and then you were challenged to be courageous for Christ in the world around you, however that might look.

SESSION SEVEN: RETREAT IS NOT AN OPTION

During this session you were challenged to not lapse in your faith but to dig your roots in even deeper. You talked about ways you can fertilize your soil to make those deep roots possible. You discussed how real faith is in continuing to walk in faith day after day, not just in spurts here and there.

HOW TO USE OVER THE EDGE

HOW IT WORKS

Over the Edge: Ultimate Submission contains seven chapters; you'll be going through one chapter a week. Each chapter revisits one session from *Dig In: The Devoted Warrior* and includes five days' worth of personal Bible studies and log entries.

You'll want to have your Bible with you as you go through each day's study. You get to dig into the Word every day and discover the truth that God has in store for you. This process will help you take the lessons of *Dig In: The Devoted Warrior* to a deeper level.

"NOTES" PAGES

At the end of each week of log entries, you'll find a couple of open pages. These are "extras" for you to use when you need more space to write or to develop your thoughts through drawings and doodles. Express yourself!

THE BUDDY SYSTEM

If you're confused by a Scripture passage, feeling convicted about something and want to talk about it, or if you just want to share how God is moving in your life (and He will move), use the buddy system. If you have an accountability partner, great! If not, bounce your ideas off a Christian friend, a youth group leader, or even—gasp!—your parents. Let them encourage you, and let them be encouraged *by* you.

STUCK?

Falling behind on your entries? Don't give up! God cares more about your heart than whether every page is filled out properly. If there's an area you feel called to linger over, linger! Take the time to listen to God instead of rushing through this journal just for the sake of completing it. But do make a commitment to developing a deeper faith in God; it won't happen on its own.

BEFORE YOU BEGIN

Take some time to pray. If you're able to be alone, pray out loud.

Jesus, I invite You into these pages. Show me Your heart, how You feel about the world and about me. Show me the shape of *my* heart. Uncover things I've hidden away and the dark corners I might not even know are there. Give me understanding as I look at Your Word and the strength to apply it to my life. Help me carve out time to meet with You every day so we can go through this together. Please come into this process, Jesus. In Your name I pray. Amen.

THE ACTIONS OF MEN are the best interpreters of their thoughts.

John Locke

WHO IS GOD? WHY SHOULD WE BE DEVOTED TO HIM? *What does devotion look like?* These were the questions you covered in your first session of *Dig In*. And your answers to these questions say a lot about your walk with God—like why you'll step out at all, what your pace will be like, and how far you will go.

This week you'll do some thinking about **WHAT IT MEANS THAT JESUS IS YOUR LORD.** As we start talking about devotion, remember this: just as words can be empty, actions can be too. Jesus doesn't want only your words of devotion. He doesn't want only your pious actions. **HE WANTS YOUR HEART.** Both of them together—words and actions—tell the world who you are and what you're about. **THE CONDITION OF YOUR HEART, DEVOTED OR DIVIDED, ALWAYS COMES OUT.**

SO WALK WITH GOD. TALK TO HIM ALONG THE WAY during this week of reflection, journaling, and prayer. **LET HIM TALK TO YOU.**

WEEK ONE DAY ONE: GOD'S GOVERNMENT

JESUS SAID, "MY KINGDOM IS NOT OF THIS WORLD. If it were, my servants would fight to prevent my arrest by the Jews. But now my kingdom is from another place."

"YOU ARE A KING, THEN!" said Pilate.

Jesus answered, "You are right in saying I am a king. In fact, for this reason I was born, and for this I came into the world, to testify to the truth. **EVERYONE ON THE SIDE OF TRUTH LISTENS TO ME."**

John 18:36–37

DURING DIG IN, you and your group created a constitution for your own country. You invented laws and policies, and you could decide how much input your citizens would have by choosing whether your country was a monarchy, oligarchy, or democracy. Whatever way you chose to run it, you had your reasons. And God has His.

You learned that the kingdom of God is not a democracy. It's a monarchy where God is in charge.

INSPECTION

Why do you think God set up His kingdom as a monarchy?

_____

_____

_____

_____

Is everyone a citizen? Is everyone subject to His rule? Is there a difference?

W1-D1

_____

_____

_____

_____

ANALYSIS

READ WHAT JESUS SAID in Matthew 25:31–46. What are the responsibilities of being a citizen in God's kingdom? What are the privileges?

_____

_____

_____

_____

Your leader mentioned that as citizens of the Kingdom, there is one truth that is central in our lives: the King is in charge! Why is this truth _central_ in our lives?

_____

_____

_____

_____

ACTION

God's kingdom is a monarchy. He doesn't have to answer to you; His rule is absolute. But does He want to hear from you? (See James 5:13–16.)

_____

_____

_____

W1-D1 DURING THIS WEEK, MEMORIZE THE FOLLOWING PASSAGE:

That if you confess with your mouth, "Jesus is Lord," and believe in your heart that God raised him from the dead, you will be saved.

Romans 10:9

HINT: To jumpstart your memory, it might be helpful to copy the verse down below. Or write it on a piece of paper, tape it to the bathroom mirror, or use it as a bookmark in a textbook.

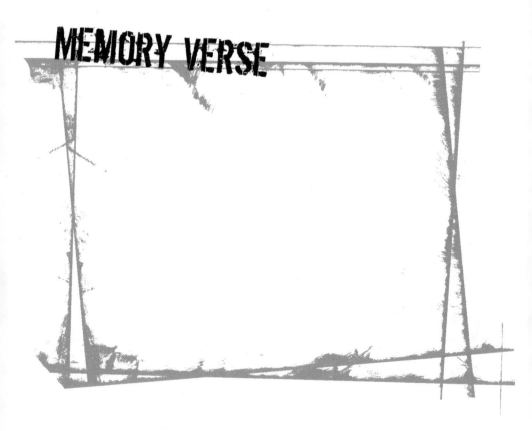

MEMORY VERSE

LORD OR LIP SERVICE?

"KNOWING THE CORRECT PASSWORD—saying, 'Master, Master,' for instance—isn't going to get you anywhere with me. What is required is serious obedience— **DOING** what my Father wills."

Matthew 7:21, MSG (emphasis added)

IN SMALL GROUPS, YOU DISCUSSED THAT "LORD" IS MORE THAN A NIFTY NICKNAME FOR GOD. When you compared the meaning of the word now to how it was used in the Middle Ages, you learned that "lord" meant "owner" or "master." And as your Training Manual mentioned, the words "lord," "owner," and "master" are interchangeable in the original Greek version of our Scripture memory verse for this week.

Let's take some time to see what it means to declare Jesus as our Lord—our owner and master.

INSPECTION

We know from the above Scripture passage that God doesn't want lip service; He wants serious obedience. What do you think obedience to God looks like in your everyday life?

_____

_____

Why is it important to be obedient in addition to declaring that Jesus is your Lord?

_____

_____

W1-D2 ANALYSIS

READ (or maybe just remember!) **ROMANS 10:9.** When you began your relationship with Jesus and confessed that He is Lord, what were you giving Him ownership over? Has anything changed in that ownership you offered? Do you offer more or less?

_____

_____

God's "owning" your life may sound negative to others (or maybe even to yourself), like you have no freedom. How can you be free if you belong to God? (See Romans 8:1–2 and James 1:25.)

_____

_____

ACTION

What are some areas of your heart that God doesn't own? They might be sins like swearing or cheating, they might be feelings you can't shake—shame, hate, or regret—or maybe it's a situation you can't get free of, like comparing yourself to someone. Stop and pray before answering. Ask God to show you what you're holding onto. Then write them down below. One at a time, ask God to become Lord over each item on your list. Then put a big, fat check mark next to each one. God's got you covered.

_____

_____

_____

_____

_____

FOLLOW ME

"MY SHEEP LISTEN to my voice; I know them, and they follow me. I give them eternal life, and they shall never perish; no one can snatch them out of my hand."

John 10:27–28

"FOLLOW ME." Funny how for some of us that phrase conjures up images of neatly bearded fishermen tossing down their nets to go hang out with Jesus. Maybe eat some bread and cure some lepers along the way. But as your peers read aloud verses from Matthew (8:20, 10:17–23, and 10:38–39), you learned that "follow me" meant a whole lot more.

HERE'S A LIST TO REFRESH YOUR MEMORY. It meant homelessness, public shame, and persecution. Now some of us might just be picturing the bearded fishermen frowning, dirty, a whole lot scruffier. Guess what? They really did suffer. **AND THE PHRASE "FOLLOW ME" HASN'T GOTTEN ANY SOFTER OR SMOOTHER BENEATH OUR FEET.** Following Jesus still means we may face the things we fear most.

INSPECTION

What are some of your fears as you follow Jesus?

_____

_____

_____

_____

What do you think you will have to face for the sake of following Him? Are you ready?

_____

_____

_____

_____

ANALYSIS

Check out the story in Acts 5:27–42. What were the apostles' attitudes about their suffering?

_____

_____

_____

_____

In verses 30–32, the apostles boldly shared the gospel message with those who were persecuting them *for sharing the gospel message*. What does that say about their courage? What does that say about their attitude toward their persecutors?

_____

_____

_____

_____

_____

Reread the verse at the top of the previous page. Think of the words as a video clip. What it looks like. What makes you feel secure as you follow Jesus?

_____

_____

_____

_____

_____

ACTION

In what ways do you think you need to be bolder in following Him?

_____

_____

_____

_____

_____

List some steps you can take to start achieving that boldness. Then, tell God how you feel about your list. Be honest.

_____

_____

_____

_____

_____

SINCE JESUS WENT THROUGH everything you're going through and more, learn to think like him. Think of your sufferings as a weaning from that old sinful habit of always expecting to get your own way. Then you'll be able to live out your days free to pursue what God wants instead of being tyrannized by what you want.

1 Peter 4:1–2, MSG

YOUR DIG IN GROUP spent some time talking about "Doubting Thomas" (John 20:24-29). So often Thomas is remembered only for his doubt, but your leader emphasized his immediate and joyful declaration of faith when he saw the risen Jesus: he cried out, "My Lord and my God!" You learned that this man dubbed "the doubter" then went on to live a life unmistakably unwavering where Christ was concerned, spreading the gospel until he died a tortuous death.

INSPECTION

Why do you think Thomas is remembered more for his doubt than his faith?

_____

_____

_____

Which aspect of his character do you relate to more?

_____

_____

_____

ANALYSIS

In Ephesians 6:13–18, Paul describes the armor God gives us, His warriors. Write down below what you think each one means and how it could be used as armor.

Belt of truth:
_____
_____
_____

Breastplate of righteousness:
_____
_____
_____

Feet fitted with readiness:
_____
_____
_____

Shield of faith:
_____
_____
_____

Helmet of salvation:
_____
_____
_____

Sword of the Spirit:
_____
_____
_____

ACTION

Has a piece of your armor gotten a little rusty? Or maybe it's

W1-D4 still fresh in the box? For each piece of armor that you've neglected to put on, list one way you can take action in that area.

_____

_____

_____

_____

Revisit your Scripture memory verse, Romans 10:9. Then think about Thomas's simple statement of devotion. What can you do every day to keep yourself centered on these basic—yet life-changing—proclamations of faith?

_____

_____

_____

_____

Talk to God about your doubts. Then repeat Thomas' statement of devotion. Listen to God and receive His encouragement and love.

_____

_____

_____

_____

_____

ONWARD!

WEEK ONE
DAY FIVE:

THE BODY IS A UNIT, though it is made up of many parts; and though all its parts are many, they form one body. So it is with Christ.

1 Corinthians 12:12

SESSION 1 of *Dig In* ended with a responsive reading of "Onward Christian Soldiers." The lyrics describe us as soldiers—warriors—like we discussed yesterday. The words are triumphant and inspiring. In fact, if we were about to play our school rival, this is the song we'd blast from the locker room.

You recited the words about the promise of victory. And it's an awesome promise, but there's another one there. The song talks about the *army* of God, not one lonely little soldier. Did you look around? Did you see that you're not alone?

INSPECTION

What type of role do you picture yourself having in God's army?

_____

_____

_____

_____

Why is it important to remember you're not alone as you charge "onward"?

_____

_____

_____

W1-D5 ANALYSIS

READ MATTHEW 18:19–20. Why do you think God set it up this way? What's so special about two or three?

_____

_____

_____

Mark 14:32–42 recounts Jesus agonizing in the Garden of Gethsemane before He is betrayed and arrested. Even though He knew He had to go to the cross alone, what does it say to you that He wanted His friends with Him as He prepared for it?

_____

_____

_____

ACTION

Look back to how you responded to the first Inspection question above. How can you carry out that role every day? How will you carry out your role with other "warriors" in God's army?

_____

_____

_____

As best you can from memory, write out your Scripture memory verse below, including the book and verse number.

_____

_____

_____

_____

NOTES

NOTES

THE LOVE OF HEAVEN
makes one heavenly.
William Shakespeare

THE SUBJECT OF LOVE has sold more record albums than any other. Love songs bring out our dramatic side; it feels satisfying to let ourselves get caught up in the thrill of falling in love and the sorrow when it ends. But is that the kind of love God talks about? Not really. There's nothing wrong with intense emotion—as long as that's not where it ends.

Your group spent time discussing in Session 2 of *Dig In* that love isn't all about feelings. In large part, **IT'S ABOUT DEVOTION AND OBEDIENCE.** Don't get me wrong, God isn't interested in icy actions totally without emotion. It's just that *feeling* something and *doing* something because of that feeling are two different things.

HE WANTS TO SEE YOUR DEVOTION. Because if He can't see it, no one else can either, and what would set you apart from the rest of the world?

GOD SHOWS HIS LOVE FOR YOU in His actions. Look how He has sustained you, guided you, and especially, saved you.

HIS LOVING ACTIONS SHOULD INSPIRE LOVING ACTIONS FROM YOU, TOO.

WEEK TWO DAY ONE: IN A NUTSHELL

"THE MOST IMPORTANT [commandment]," answered Jesus, **"is this: 'Hear, O Israel, the Lord our God, the Lord is one. Love the Lord your God with all your heart and with all your soul and with all your mind and with all your strength.' The second is this: 'Love your neighbor as yourself.' There is no commandment greater than these."**

Mark 12:29–31

REMEMBER GETTING TOGETHER with your group to try to come up with a one-sentence motto of what it means to be a Christian? It's pretty tough; it seems like there's so much we should cover. Don't worry. Jesus broke it down for us: *love God with everything you've got, and love each other.*

INSPECTION

Do you remember the motto you wrote? How did it compare to the one Jesus gave us?

_____

_____

_____

Does this motto make you feel like you know what God expects from you? Why or why not?

_____

_____

ANALYSIS

The Message puts Romans 13:8 this way: "Don't run up debts, except for the huge debt of love you owe each other. When you love others, you complete what the law has been after all along." So, okay. We're supposed to love each other, but what does that really mean? Read 1 Corinthians 13:4–7. What stands out to you the most about how we should love?

_____

_____

_____

ACTION

We often look at 1 Corinthians 13:4–7 as a portrait of how our human love relationships are supposed to work. But shouldn't it be a guidepost for how we should love God, too? Below you'll find principles from the 1 Corinthians passage reworded into questions. The "self-checks" are there just to get the wheels turning; don't limit yourself to them. When you come to each one, think about if you're loving God the way the Bible explains love. If not, next to it, write a one-sentence confession of how your love has fallen short.

Are you **patient** with God? *(Self-check: How long do you wait for an answer to prayer before giving up?)*_____

_____

_____

_____

Are you **kind** to God? *(Self-check: Do you compliment your friends more than you compliment God?)* _____

_____

_____

_____

Are you **prideful** toward God? *(Self-check: Do you rely on your own intelligence and reasoning skills or do you look to God?)*

_____

_____

_____

W2-D1 Are you **rude** to God? *(Self-check: Do you blow God off for days without talking to Him?)* _____

_____

_____

Are you **self-seeking** toward God? *(Self-check: How much of your prayers' "want lists" have to do with God's glory and purposes?)*

_____

_____

Do you get **angry** with God? *(Self-check: Do you keep track of when He hasn't done things your way and hold it against Him?)*

_____

_____

Do you **take pleasure** in evil? *(Self-check: Are there sins you like to take part in?)* _____

_____

_____

Do you **protect** God? *(Self-check: Do you stand up for Him?)*

_____

_____

Do you **trust** God? *(Self-check: Do you trust that He is really all you need?)* _____

_____

_____

Is your **hope** in God? *(Self-check: Do you put hope in your ability to do things? And a serious salvation question: Do you put a lot of stock in the fact that you're a "good person," or is your hope for salvation in Jesus alone?)* _____

_____

_____

Do you **persevere** with God? *(Self-check: How do you respond when you're having dry times in your faith?)* _____

_____

_____

HEARTTHROB

WEEK TWO
DAY TWO

"AND YOU, MY SON SOLOMON, acknowledge the God of your father, and serve him with wholehearted devotion and with a willing mind, for the LORD searches every heart and understands every motive behind the thoughts."

1 Chronicles 28:9a

REMEMBER HOW your leader molded a lump of clay into a heart? The heart probably didn't look like it came out of a pressing machine. There were lumps, some thin edges, and maybe even imprints where your leader's fingernails dug in a little deeper.

You also may have noticed that he or she didn't touch a spot just once and call it done. There were some spots that took some special care to form, like the two gentle arches at the top and where it came to a point at the bottom. And the same is true with God. Some parts of your heart might take a few trips through God's fingertips before it takes on the shape He wants. But don't be discouraged; only leave your heart in His hands.

INSPECTION

In what ways can you feel God molding your heart to love Him and others more? Give an example. _____

_____

_____

_____

_____

OVER THE EDGE: ULTIMATE SUBMISSION   33

Are there areas you feel like He's *remolded* and remolded? If so, what are they? _____

_____

_____

ANALYSIS

READ EZEKIEL 11:19–21. What does it mean to have an "undivided heart"? How can you compare a "heart of flesh" to the clay heart we've been talking about?

_____

_____

_____

_____

Draw a heart and divide it into two sections: the part wholly devoted to God and the part still following the world. Which section is bigger?

_____

_____

_____

Look at your Scripture memory verse on the next page, Mark 12:30–31, and look up Psalm 73:25–26. Let's put these two thoughts together: "Love the Lord your God with all your heart . . . and with all your strength" and "God is the strength of my heart." Who is at the center of your ability to love God? Why does loving God take strength? Who gives you that strength?

_____

_____

_____

ACTION

Along with the psalmist, pray the words of Psalm 139:23–24.

_____

_____

Memorize the motto Jesus gave us, Mark 12:30–31.

"LOVE THE LORD YOUR GOD with all your heart and with all your soul and with all your mind and with all your strength. The second is this: Love your neighbor as yourself. There is no commandment greater than these."

Mark 12:30–31

Remember how your leader mentioned that the Israelites used to post this all over the place so that they would be constantly reminded? Consider doing the same! (Start by writing it below.)

MEMORY VERSE

WEEK TWO DAY THREE: WILLFUL AND READY

"IF YOU LOVE ME, you will obey what I command."
John 14:15.

YESTERDAY WE LOOKED AT HOW GOD is molding our hearts to love Him and those around us and that it is a process. Today we'll think about how it is a *willful* process on your part. God's hands are open, soft, and pliable as He molds your heart; they aren't clenched in a kung-fu grip around you. It's your choice to leave your heart in His hands.

Your leader may have used another visual image to get this point across, such as how we aren't made to obey God like a dog led around on a leash or like He is holding the video game controller and we are characters on the screen. It's all about our choice to follow Him.

INSPECTION

What makes obedience an expression of love?

_____

_____

_____

_____

Why did God make obedience optional?

_____

_____

_____

ANALYSIS

READ GENESIS 2:15-17. Why did God give Adam and Eve access to the tree of good and evil?

_____

_____

_____

Isaiah chapter 6 starts by telling about a vision that Isaiah had. Read verses 1–8. What do you notice about verse 8—how does God seek out Isaiah's obedience (does He demand it)? How does Isaiah respond?

_____

_____

_____

ACTION

Your obedience to God is a way to show your love for Him. Using these categories from your Scripture memory verse, write down a way you can be obedient in each area.

_____

_____

_____

How can I be obedient with my...
heart & soul _____

_____

mind _____

_____

strength _____

_____

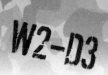

Tell God what's in your heart about obedience. Express your love to Him.

_____

_____

_____

_____

_____

_____

SURRENDER ALL

THEREFORE, I URGE YOU, BROTHERS, in view of God's mercy, to offer your bodies as living sacrifices, holy and pleasing to God—this is your spiritual act of worship.

Romans 12:1

EARLIER THIS WEEK, we summed up our Scripture memory verse—our motto—in this way: love God with everything you've got and love each other. During Session 2 of *Dig In*, your leader named an area of your life, and then asked you how you could show your love for God in that area. Let's review that list.

How can you love God with your ___(fill in a word from below)__?

_____

_____

Time   Friend Relationships
Money   Dreams
Schoolwork   Dating Relationships
Family Relationships   Life
Hobbies

INSPECTION

Have you made a conscious effort to love God with the areas of your life that your leader mentioned?

_____

_____

_____

If so, how's it going? If not, what's holding you back?

_____

_____

_____

ANALYSIS

Check out 1 John 2:15–17. Other than the fact that God deserves all our love, why should we not waste our love on things in this world?

_____

_____

_____

We shouldn't love the things of this world more than God, but we can turn the things of this world that we're involved in into an offering of love. Reread Romans 12:1 at the top of the previous page. Do you think Paul is talking only about our physical bodies? If not, what else could he be talking about?

_____

_____

_____

ACTION

From the list on the previous page, select two areas in which you most struggle to show your love to God. It might help to think about our discussion yesterday—how showing obedience is also showing love. Journal specifically (make a plan) about how you can show love and obedience in those areas. Then talk to God about your plan and your desires to obey and love Him.

_____

_____

_____

THE LORD YOUR GOD is with you, he is mighty to save. He will take great delight in you, he will quiet you with his love, he will rejoice over you with singing.

Zephaniah 3:17

YOU SPENT A LOT OF TIME LEARNING about how we ought to love God and to show that love through devotion and obedience. We also know from our memory verse that it is crucial that we love those around us the way we want to be loved. But what makes it possible for us—with our natural tendency to be selfish—to lavish love on God and others?

INSPECTION

On a scale of 1–10, how easy do you find it to love others? Why do you think that is?

_____

_____

_____

_____

_____

How easy is it to love God on a scale of 1–10? Why is that?

_____

_____

_____

_____

_____

_____

W2-D5 ANALYSIS

What makes us able to love God and love others? See I John 4:9–21.

_____

_____

_____

_____

_____

_____

READ DEUTERONOMY 7:7–9. What does it mean that there is a covenant of love (a binding promise) between us and God?

_____

_____

_____

_____

_____

_____

What does it say about God that He would make a covenant of love with us in the first place? What is our responsibility in this covenant?

_____

_____

_____

_____

_____

_____

ACTION

God loves you in an awesome way. Take some time to write a love letter to God. Start it out by writing, "I love you, Lord, because . . ."

_____

_____

_____

_____

_____

_____

_____

_____

_____

_____

_____

_____

_____

_____

_____

_____

_____

_____

As best as you can, write down the memory verse—the motto Jesus gave us to live by—below.

_____

_____

_____

_____

_____

_____

_____

_____

NOTES

NOTES

THE MEN WHO FOLLOWED HIM were unique in their generation. They turned the world upside down because their hearts had been turned right side up. The world has never been the same.

Billy Graham

WANT TO TAKE THE WORLD BY STORM?

It's simple. You've gotta keep the story of the cross close to your heart. It has to become part of the life-force pumping through your veins, the air you breathe in and out, the power in putting one foot in front of the other. Let it be the center of your speech and your movement.

When you stay close to this amazing story of God's faithfulness, **YOU WILL RESPOND IN FAITHFULNESS;** you will respond with the phrase you became familiar with during *Dig In,*

"I AM YOURS FOREVER!"

CARRYING HIS OWN CROSS, he went out to the place of the Skull (which in Aramaic is called Golgotha). Here they crucified him, and with him two others—one on each side and Jesus in the middle.

John 19:17–18

REMEMBER THE SCAVENGER HUNT your group did? You searched all over the building for symbols of things like *commitment, faith, love, and friendship?* The cross can symbolize those same positive ideas since through Jesus' *commitment* to saving us we can enter into a *loving friendship* with Him when we have faith. But it also tells a violent story; it symbolizes the brutality Jesus went through to put us right with Him.

INSPECTION

When you see a cross, what comes to mind first—what we gain from the cross or what Jesus went through on the cross?

_____

_____

_____

How do you feel about seeing crosses used in jewelry, home décor, and even in churches? Do you think they diminish the message of the cross or are they powerful visual reminders? Why?

_____

_____

_____

_____

ANALYSIS

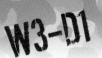

Symbol = something that stands for, represents, or suggests another thing. (Webster's Dictionary)

_____

_____

_____

_____

Even before His crucifixion, Jesus sets up the cross as a symbol. (See Matthew 16:24.) Why do you think Jesus wanted His disciples to see the cross as a symbol? What does it represent in this passage?

_____

_____

_____

CHECK OUT ISAIAH 8:18. What do you think it means

that *we*, as God's people, are signs and symbols? (See the dictionary definition above if you need a hint.)

_____

_____

_____

_____

ACTION

Think about that last question. How can you better carry out your role as God's symbol?

_____

_____

_____

_____

W3-D1

This week, memorize the following verse and its reference. In the space below, draw what it will look like in your life to "take up your cross."

THEN JESUS SAID TO HIS DISCIPLES, "If anyone would come after me, he must deny himself and take up his cross and follow me."

Matthew 16:24

MEMORY VERSE

JESUS SAID, "It is finished."
John 19:30

Betrayed.
Abandoned.
Mocked.
Stripped.
Whipped.
Crowned.
Impaled.
Displayed.
Cramped.
Suffocated.
Entombed.
Raised.

Finished.

INSPECTION

What did Jesus "finish" on the cross?

_____

_____

_____

_____

How does it make you feel that Jesus would go to the cross on purpose and on your behalf?

_____

_____

_____

_____

W3-D2 ANALYSIS

READ MARK'S VERSION of the crucifixion story, chapter 15. What sticks out to you most in the story (what is the most compelling part for you)?

_____

_____

Mark 15:38 talks about the curtain of the temple. The curtain of the temple was the entrance to the Holy of Holies, a place where only high priests could go once a year to be in God's presence. What does Mark 15:38 mean for us as Christians? (Read Hebrews 9 if you'd like more explanation.)

_____

_____

ACTION

Try to picture yourself at the scene of the crucifixion. You're watching Jesus hang on a hill in the afternoon's scorching heat. Streaks of blood and sweat stream down His face. He puts all His weight on the nail going through His feet to push up for a gasp of air and then sinks down, dangling from the nails in His hands. And all you can do is watch. He looks down at you and meets your eye. What does He say? What do you say? Close your eyes to imagine it, then respond.

_____

_____

Take some time to thank Jesus for the work He did on the cross.

_____

_____

WHY??

FOR THE WAGES OF SIN is death, but the gift of God
is eternal life in Christ Jesus our Lord.

Romans 6:23

WHY DID JESUS HAVE TO DIE? Volunteers from your
group read verses like John 3:16, Romans 5:6–11, and the verse
above. You're encouraged to look these verses up and go over
them a time or two. They are so fundamentally important
because they talk about our need for a Savior.

So we know we needed to be cleansed of our sin. But why the
blood bath of the cross? Why did blood have to be involved to
put us right with God again, sparing us from an eternity apart
from Him? Let's try to find some answers.

INSPECTION

What do you think an eternity apart from God would look like?
What would it feel like?

_____

_____

For people who are living apart from God in their lives right
now, do you think they are feeling the full force of what hell will
be? How would it be the same or different, depending on how
you answered?

_____

_____

_____

W3-D3 ANALYSIS

After Adam and Eve sinned in the Garden of Eden, God clothed them with animal skins to cover the shame they felt when they realized they were naked (Gen. 3:21). Man sinned, and the first animal's blood flowed because of it. How is the sacrifice of Jesus kind of like a skin covering our shame?

_____

_____

_____

Later, God made it part of the Law in the Old Testament to make animal sacrifices every year to atone (make amends) for sin. Check out Leviticus 17:11—what's so special about blood?

_____

_____

_____

Leviticus 22:19–20 says that the animal had to be without "defect" to be acceptable; it had to be perfect. Connect that requirement with Jesus—what do you see?

_____

_____

_____

ACTION

It's no coincidence that the Passover was the setting for the crucifixion. Exodus 12 tells the story of the first Passover, when the Israelites were supposed to sacrifice a lamb (without defect, of course) and smear the blood above their doorway. Then when God saw that the satisfactory sacrifice had been made, He would pass over their house and spare the people inside. When you ask Jesus to be your Savior, it sounds weird, but what you're doing is asking Him to mark your doorway with His perfect blood.

Draw a house below. Mark the doorway with a cross—the symbol of the ultimate sacrifice. Then either draw figures or write the names of people you want to be sure are safe with you in the house—saved by Jesus' blood.

Pray about the people outside your "house." Let God lead you as you pray and ask what He wants of you.

_____

_____

_____

THE RIGHT REACTION

HOW CAN I REPAY THE LORD for all his goodness to me? I will lift up the cup of salvation and call on the name of the LORD. I will fulfill my vows to the Lord in the presence of all his people.

Psalm 116:12–14

FROM THE TIME YOU WERE LITTLE, your parents would prompt you to say "thank you" when someone gave you a gift—"What do you sa-a-ay?" The point was that kindness deserves adequate response.

You watched a video clip where a guy named Edmond could have killed a prisoner named Jacapo, but he decides to save his life instead. Jacapo reacts by gratefully vowing, "I am your man forever!" Jesus decided to save our lives, too, at great personal cost to Himself. So what do you sa-a-ay?

INSPECTION

The very first time you heard about what Jesus did for you on the cross, how did you respond?

_____

_____

_____

_____

What is your response every time you hear the story again? Has it lost its power on you at all, like you've heard it a million times, or is it like hearing it afresh each time? Does its "grip" on you affect how close you feel to the Lord?

W3-D4

ANALYSIS

Luke 17:11–17 tells how Jesus healed 10 lepers. How many of them responded with utter gratitude? What do you think that says about our tendency as humans? Which group do you see yourself in?

In Matthew 13:53–58, the people of Nazareth, Jesus' hometown, can't see past His being the boy next door. What does their faithless response hinder Him from doing?

ACTION

In your own words, tell Jesus, "I am yours forever!" Write down key words from your thoughts.

W3-D4 **RE-READ THE VERSE** at the top page 58. What would it look like for you to fulfill your vow in front of His people?

_____

_____

_____

_____

Now talk to God. Tell Him, "I am yours forever." Express your heart and mind to the Father.

_____

_____

_____

_____

_____

_____

_____

_____

FOUR LITTLE WORDS

[JESUS] ASKED, "Who do you say that I am?" Simon Peter answered, "You are the Christ, the Son of the living God."

JESUS REPLIED, "BLESSED ARE YOU, Simon son of Jonah, for this was not revealed to you by man, but by my Father in heaven."

Matthew 16:15b–17

YOUR GROUP DISCUSSED HOW those four words— "You are the Christ"—were life-changing words for Peter. It was a simple statement of faith, but when Peter heard Jesus' response—telling him that he was blessed and that he was *tapped into the Father,* Peter must have felt pretty pleased with himself. He probably looked proudly around at the other disciples, straightening his smock and smiling. After all, Jesus was sometimes irritated with His disciples for not understanding His parables and teachings, always having to explain what they meant. And here Peter says something right on the money without being coached!

But it was only a moment before his bubble burst. Here comes our memory verse: Jesus tells Peter to take up his own cross if he wants to follow Him.

W3-D5 INSPECTION

Peter probably frowned when he heard what Jesus told him he would have to do. How do you react to God's telling you to do the same?

_____

_____

_____

_____

ANALYSIS

READ THE WHOLE PASSAGE OF MATTHEW 16:13–28. Jesus called Peter "blessed" in one breath and "Satan" in the next. What is Satan-like about having your mind on the things of men?

_____

_____

_____

_____

What does it mean to deny yourself and take up your cross?

_____

_____

_____

_____

Taking up a cross seems like a big lug of responsibility and hardship. How can we look at it in light of Matthew 11:28–30? Do these two passages contradict each other? Why or why not?

_____

_____

_____

ACTION

In what specific way is God calling you to deny yourself?

_____
_____
_____

Talk to Him about it.

_____
_____
_____
_____

Write the Scripture memory verse below with its reference.

_____
_____
_____
_____
_____
_____

NOTES

NOTES

THE GREATEST TRICK the Devil ever pulled was convincing the world he didn't exist.

Charles Baudelaire

SESSION 4 PROBABLY MADE SATAN a very real person to you; you defined him as God's enemy and as one who hates you and hates God. And that's exactly what Satan was afraid of. He's an enemy! Enemies don't want their presence known as they try to infiltrate territory! Staying low to the ground, sneaky and slithery—that's the way Satan wants to invade your heart.

SATAN WOULD LIKE YOU to think that it's only weird, over-the-top people who talk about his role on this earth. He would love for everyone to forget about him, push him to the back of the closet like something unfashionable your Great Aunt Frieda gave you.

But this week we're gonna **CALL SATAN ON THE CARPET;** we'll talk about hating him and the things in the world he would like to trip us up with. And we'll talk about passionately loving our God.

GET READY TO DIVE INTO LOVE AND HATE AND WHAT IT ALL MEANS!

WEEK FOUR DAY ONE: THE BIG TIME

THEY OVERCAME HIM BY THE BLOOD of the Lamb and by the word of their testimony; they did not love their lives so much as to shrink from death. Therefore rejoice, you heavens and you who dwell in them! But woe to the earth and the sea, because the devil has gone down to you! He is filled with fury, because he knows that his time is short.

Revelation 12:11–12

DURING THE GAME OF "TEAM BLOB TAG," if you were tagged by "IT," you had to join his side and try to tag your former teammates. Well, the world is like Team Blob Tag except that this is the big time—the pros, the show! At the end, it will matter for all eternity whose team you're on. And you better believe that Satan is trying to tag you—and get you to help him take down the other side.

INSPECTION

Since we don't have the luxury of everybody being marked with or without a masking tape "X" on their shirt like in Team Blob Tag, how can you tell if someone is on your team or the enemy's team?

_____

_____

_____

_____

_____

Is it clear to others whose team *you're* on?

_____

_____

_____

_____

_____

ANALYSIS

READ JOB 2:1-10. When God asks Satan where he has just come from, what do you think Satan's answer means? Read also 1 Peter 5:8.

_____

_____

_____

_____

Why did God let Satan inflict pain on Job (look to verses 4 and 5)? (Look to James 1:12 for another hint.)

_____

_____

_____

_____

_____

_____

Being on God's team is more than just believing that He exists. See James 2:19. What is the difference between *believing that Jesus died on the cross* for our sins and *putting faith* in that fact?

_____

_____

_____

_____

W4-D1 ACTION

Meditate on and memorize the following verse.

"Everyone who does evil hates the light, and will not come into the light for fear that his deeds will be exposed."

John 3:20

Begin memorizing by writing out the verse below.

MEMORY VERSE

THERE IS A TIME FOR EVERYTHING, and a season for every activity under heaven...a time to love and a time to hate.

Ecclesiastes 3:1, 8a

HATE WHAT IS EVIL; cling to what is good.

Romans 12:9b

IF YOU THOUGHT "HATE" shouldn't be part of your Christian vocabulary, you found out you were dead-wrong. As your *Dig In* leader named a band, food, or movie, you could only hold up your black or red construction paper heart to signify love or hate; there was no neutral territory.

And God feels the same way. Either you're for Him or against Him. Either you hate Satan and his works, or you love him. God leaves the choice up to you.

INSPECTION

How does God feel about you? How does Satan feel about you?

_____

_____

_____

_____

How do you feel about God? How do you feel about Satan?

_____

_____

_____

_____

ANALYSIS

Keeping this love/hate idea in mind, how do you see that standard in our Scripture memory verse? The latter part of the verse is often associated with non-Christians, but can you also associate it with a Christian's hesitation to confess sin?

_____

_____

_____

LOOK UP JOHN 12:23–25. What does it mean to hate your life in this world? How would you explain the first part of this passage about the kernel of wheat in light of Galatians 2:20, which says, "I have been crucified [killed] with Christ"?

_____

_____

_____

_____

ACTION

Deuteronomy 7:26 says, "Do not bring a detestable thing into your house or you, like it, will be set apart for destruction. Utterly abhor and detest it, for it is set apart for destruction."

_____

_____

_____

_____

Last week you drew a Passover house and the people you wanted to be safe inside with you. This time when you draw a house, draw symbols representing "detestable things" being tossed out the windows. In the Old Testament, this meant things that were defiled or unclean according to Jewish Law, but think of it today as a sin that's holed up in your "house" or even an object that isn't glorifying to God, such as a CD or movie you own. Then, start housecleaning!

WEEK FOUR DAY THREE: CLOUDY GRAY

THEREFORE, SINCE WE ARE SURROUNDED by such a great cloud of witnesses, let us throw off everything that hinders and the sin that so easily entangles, and let us run with perseverance the race marked out for us.

Hebrews 12:1

THE BIBLE DOESN'T GIVE us exact guidelines on every aspect of our lives, whether we should love something or hate it. But as you discussed with your group, you can use the Bible to help you determine how you should feel about an issue. Hold on to the passages you discussed to help you weed through the areas that aren't exactly black and white. They were Philippians 4:4–8 and Galatians 5:19–24. And let's look at some more verses that might be helpful.

INSPECTION

Have you tried to use the passages you discussed with your group (Phil. 4:4–8 & Gal. 5:19–24) to help you figure out the gray areas you've come across? If so, have they helped? If not, look them up again and ask God to write them on your heart, calling them to mind when you're faced with a gray area.

_____
_____
_____
_____
_____
_____

_____

_____

ANALYSIS

Next to each reference, write down the gist of what the verse is saying and reword it into a guideline to live by.

Hebrews 10:24

_____
_____
_____

Romans 12:18

_____
_____
_____

1 Peter 1:14

_____
_____
_____

ACTION

As you think about "gray" (it doesn't seem black or white) activities and relationships, keep in mind that those are the ones we seldom like to put into the light, like our Scripture memory verse says we should. It's easy to think that because you aren't 100% sure if it's wrong, you won't be held accountable for it. Think again. Take some time to evaluate the gray areas you might have been glossing over. Does God want you to deal with them? Just to get you started, think about your . . .

W4-D3 …clothes (Are you totally modest? Are you materialistic about it? Does what you wear honor God?)

_____

_____

_____

…language (Maybe you don't technically swear, but do you say borderline words that have the feel of the world's language? Are crude or questionable comments a part of your speech?)

_____

_____

_____

…conversation (Do you brag? Talk behind someone's back? Make sarcastic comments?) _____

_____

_____

…free time (Relaxing is good and necessary, but how much of your free time is spent that way?)_____

_____

_____

…money (Do you share? Are you greedy?) _____

_____

_____

…relationships (Are you in one for selfish reasons?) _____

_____

_____

…other areas _____

_____

_____

Now offer yourself, through prayer, to God. Give Him an opportunity to confirm what He wants you to understand. Praise Him from your heart.

PASSION FOR THE CHRIST

"IF ANYONE COMES TO ME and does not hate his father and mother, his wife and children, his brothers and sisters—yes, even his own life—he cannot be my disciple."

Luke 14:26

WOW, JESUS DOESN'T MESS AROUND! That's probably how you responded at first when your *Dig In* leader read the passage above. Calling us to hate our families? It seems so…un-Jesus. But as you found out, Jesus was using a strong exaggeration to communicate the idea that, when compared with our enormous love for God, our love for family looks like hate. Let's continue to examine this challenging passage.

INSPECTION

Is your love for God so extreme that the love for your family looks like hate? If not, why do you think you've put your family on equal footing with God in your life?

_____

_____

_____

_____

_____

Why do you think God wants extreme love from you?

_____

_____

_____

_____

W4-D4 ANALYSIS

READ THE STORY IN LUKE 9:57–62. What does this passage teach us about how quickly God wants us to respond to His call? How about the impermanence of earth-life versus the eternity of God's kingdom?

_____

_____

_____

_____

Part of our love for something is our dependence on it. What does Jeremiah 17:5 have to say about depending on humans? What direction are our hearts facing when we are depending on people (for love, acceptance, direction—you name it!) instead of God?

_____

_____

_____

_____

ACTION

Having an impassioned love for God—leaps and bounds more than we love the people closest to us—can seem pretty hard since we can't physically see Him. Sometimes it can be hard to even have faith, given the pulls of the world we live in and the efforts of our enemy, Satan.

_____

_____

_____

Below you'll find a list of words. Next to each one, \textbf{W4-D4} journal about how by using each word, you can culti- vate a crazy-in-love-with-Jesus kind of love. (Remember that the reason you can love God at all is that He first loved you. So ask for His power as you endeavor to love Him more.)

Bible reading _____
_____
_____

The Holy Spirit _____
_____
_____

Your past _____
_____
_____

Your future _____
_____
_____

Time _____
_____
_____

Listening prayer _____
_____
_____

Hardships _____
_____
_____

Blessings _____
_____
_____

REJECT & RENOUNCE

SO, IF YOU THINK YOU ARE standing firm, be careful that you don't fall! No temptation has seized you except what is common to man. And God is faithful; he will not let you be tempted beyond what you can bear. But when you are tempted, he will also provide a way out so that you can stand up under it.

1 Corinthians 10:12–13

AT THE END OF THE FOURTH SESSION of *Dig In,* you taped your black heart to the banner filled with the world's values, and then you turned your back on it to symbolize turning away from Satan and his lies. You said out loud that you renounce the devil and his empty promises. Since the Holy Spirit is in you, you have dominion over Satan. Whatever he is dishing your way, *you don't have to take it!*

INSPECTION

After you verbally renounced Satan, did you notice if he tried to tempt you even more, or did it get easier for a while?

_____

_____

_____

Did turning your back on Satan turn you toward God more?

_____

_____

_____

ANALYSIS

LOOK UP LUKE 4:40–41. Why wouldn't Jesus want the demons to be the ones to tell everyone who He is?

_____

_____

_____

Read about the 72 messengers Jesus sent out in Luke 10:1–21. What does it mean to be like lambs among wolves—who are the lambs and why are they compared to lambs? Who are the wolves and why are they compared to wolves?

_____

_____

_____

In that same passage, verses 18–20 talk about our authority over Satan. What does Jesus say about how we should feel about having that dominion?

_____

_____

_____

ACTION

The Bible verse at the top of the page promises that there is a way out of temptation, even if it feels like it's closing in on you, God says you can stand up to it! Brainstorm what you can do to stand up under Satan's temptation and write them below.

_____

_____

_____

_____

W4-D5 To encourage you to keep yourself in God's light and expose (confess to God) the dark deeds that the devil has drawn you to, keep the Scripture memory verse in your mind. Take the time to write it below.

_____

_____

_____

_____

_____

_____

Confess anything wrong you've done, and let God clean your heart and mind and draw you completely into the light, with Him.

_____

_____

_____

_____

_____

_____

_____

NOTES

NOTES

HUMANS ARE AMPHIBIANS—half spirit and half animal. As spirits they belong to the eternal world, but as animals they inhabit time.

C. S. Lewis

THIS WEEK WE'LL EXPLORE SOMETHING that you touched on during the fifth session of *Dig In*. Basically, it's this: this isn't home, but here we are.

FOR THOSE OF US WHOSE HEARTS HAVE BEEN LABELED like a book in the library ("This soul belongs to Jesus"), we feel a little out of place here. Our morals don't match the world's morals. The way we think about things from—hopefully!—God's perspective is in direct disagreement with the way the world thinks about things.

BUT NO MATTER HOW OUT OF WHACK THE WORLD IS, AND no matter how strong or weak, confident or unsure you might feel, there's a reason you're here.

AND IN THAT SENSE, YES, YOU DO BELONG.

SET APART HEARTS

BUT IN YOUR HEARTS set apart Christ as Lord. Always be prepared to give an answer to everyone who asks you to give the reason for the hope that you have. But do this with gentleness and respect, keeping a clear conscience, so that those who speak maliciously against your good behavior in Christ may be ashamed of their slander.

1 Peter 3:15–16

YOU LISTENED TO JOE PISTONE'S story, how his undercover assignment as an FBI agent was to blend into a mafia organization in order to bring malicious crooks to justice. A noble ending but with a hefty pricetag: blurring the line of *pretending* to be a criminal versus *internalizing* a criminal mind-set.

As you hang out with your non-Christian friends, you'll need to be careful not to do the same. Remember Team Blob Tag? It should be as clear to everyone whose team you're on that it's as if you were wearing a masking tape "X" on your shirt.

INSPECTION

Have you ever given in to the pressure to blend in and, in the process, compromised your faith values?

_____

_____

_____

_____

_____

_____

Where does that pressure come from (Satan, society, peers, yourself?), and why is it risky to give in to it?

_____
_____
_____
_____
_____
_____

ANALYSIS

READ GALATIANS 1:10. Put the last part, "If I were still trying to please men, I would not be a servant of Christ," into your own words. What does this have to do with being set apart—not looking like or acting like—the world?

_____
_____
_____
_____
_____
_____

READ 1 SAMUEL 8:19–22. Then, read the price for wanting to be like "other nations" in 1 Samuel 8:10–18, which is exactly what ended up happening. What does this story have to teach us about fitting in versus doing it God's way?

_____
_____
_____
_____
_____
_____

W5-D1 ACTION

List below three actions that will show the world that you are set apart.

_____

_____

_____

Memorize the following verse this week. It's hefty, but it's worth the time and effort to write it on your heart.

NOW THIS IS OUR BOAST: Our conscience testifies that we have conducted ourselves in the world, and especially in our relations with you, in the holiness and sincerity that are from God. We have done so not according to worldly wisdom but according to God's grace.

2 Corinthians 1:12

Try praying this verse daily, letting God ingrain His words in you.

MEMORY VERSE

WHAT A WORLD!

THE GOD WHO MADE THE WORLD and everything in it is the Lord of heaven and earth and does not live in temples built by hands. And he is not served by human hands, as if he needed anything, because he himself gives all men life and breath and everything else. From one man he made every nation of men, that they should inhabit the whole earth.... God did this so that men would seek him and perhaps reach out for him and find him, though he is not far from each one of us.

Acts 17:24–27

YESTERDAY WE TALKED about being set apart from the world, and last week we talked about hating the world. It sounds like you shouldn't touch anything in the world with a 10-foot pole, right? Yes and no. The point is this: don't get caught up in the self-pleasing stuff of this place, and stay clear of Satan's traps, *but love the people here.* Love the sinners—you were one not too long ago, weren't you?

God's fed up with all the sin we're mired in down here, but that doesn't mean He wouldn't still send His only Son wading into the muck to save those who are sinking.

INSPECTION

You've probably heard the phrase, "Hate the sin; love the sinner." What does that mean to you, and how does it apply here?

_____

_____

_____

_____

What one word would you use to describe the world?

_____

ANALYSIS

Jesus hung out with riff-raff; read Mark 2:13–17. Maybe He spoke truth into their lives at some point, but notice verse 15. Is He preaching at them? What insight does this give you about what kind of relationship we should have with the world?

_____

_____

_____

_____

READ REVELATION 3:20. What does this passage, in which God is pursuing a relationship, tell you about His love for the sinful world? What, according to this passage, needs to be done on our part?

_____

_____

_____

_____

ACTION

This week, with the Holy Spirit's leading, make an effort to have a conversation with someone about spiritual things. With gentleness and respect (like the verse at the top of the page said yesterday), feel free to share your faith. But focus *first* on exercising your listening skills. Listen to them. Let them formulate their ideas and try to put them into words. They'll be much more likely to want to stay in the conversation if you show them their thoughts are valued.

HOME

"IF THE WORLD HATES YOU, keep in mind that it hated me first. If you belonged to the world, it would love you as its own. As it is, you do not belong to the world, but I have chosen you out of the world. That is why the world hates you."

John 15:18–19

YOUR GROUP TALKED ABOUT how our true citizenship is with God in heaven. Maybe you've even felt that in your spirit, like you don't quite belong here. And it's not just because the world is a sinful place like we've been talking about. There's another reason we'll explore.

INSPECTION

Have you ever felt like the world is a foreign place to you? Describe why and how.

_____
_____
_____
_____
_____

Do you think people who are unsaved feel that way at all? Why or why not?

_____
_____
_____
_____
_____

W5-D3 ANALYSIS

The world doesn't feel like our home only because the world resists us and we resist the world. Read Psalm 84:2. How do the words of this verse illustrate how we don't feel at home here?

_____

_____

_____

_____

Acts 17:28 says, "For in him we live and move and have our being." What does this tell you about where our true home is?

_____

_____

_____

_____

ACTION

Besides through prayer, how can you tap into your home?

_____

_____

_____

_____

How can you turn feeling not at home, which can feel lonely, into something good?

_____

_____

_____

_____

_____

SHINY

"HERE'S ANOTHER WAY TO PUT IT: You're here to be light, bringing out the God-colors in the world. God is not a secret to be kept. We're going public with this, as public as a city on a hill. If I make you light-bearers, you don't think I'm going to hide you under a bucket, do you? I'm putting you on a light stand. Now that I've put you there on a hilltop, on a light stand—shine! Keep open house; be generous with your lives. By opening up to others, you'll prompt people to open up with God, this generous Father in heaven."

Matthew 5:14–16, MSG

WHILE THIS WORLD IS NOT OUR HOME, there's no denying that we're going to live here for a while. What we do with our time is important. During *Dig In,* you discussed that God's mission for us has two parts: the first focuses on how we should live and the second on what we are to do. Let's take 'em one at a time, starting with how we are to live in a way that shows others who God is.

INSPECTION

How does the way you live your life show others *who God is?*

_____

_____

_____

Is that what *your* life is showing?

_____

_____

_____

W5-D4 ANALYSIS

READ PSALM 39:4-6. Are you "bustling about"? Is it a deep, dark goal to "heap up wealth"? How does knowing the briefness of your life influence the way you live it?

_____

_____

_____

What are the two key words from our Scripture memory verse that describe how we should conduct ourselves? What do they mean to you?

_____

_____

_____

ACTION

How can you put those two key words from the memory verse into action in your daily life? Be specific and realistic.

_____

_____

_____

The memory verse talks about your conscience. Is it clear? Ask Jesus to show you if you have conducted yourself in the way you should. Take some time to confess if you haven't, and for the times you've been "successful," thank Him for doing His good work through you.

_____

_____

_____

_____

SHOW & TELL

WE ARE THEREFORE CHRIST'S AMBASSADORS, as though God were making his appeal through us. We implore you on Christ's behalf: Be reconciled to God.

2 Corinthians 5:20

TODAY WE'LL DISCUSS THE SECOND PART of Christ's mission for us: what we are to do here. Your leader talked about how, while it is very important to live an upright life, you could live a good life for 80 years, but if you never *tell* anyone about Jesus, you've failed and they're in for an eternity of hurt.

INSPECTION

Is it more, less, or equally important to *tell about Jesus* as compared to *showing Him* through the way you live your life? Why?

_____

_____

_____

_____

_____

Which do you put more emphasis on in your life: showing or telling?

_____

_____

_____

_____

_____

W5-D5 ANALYSIS

Jude 22–23a says this: "Be merciful to those who doubt; snatch others from the fire and save them . . . ." These verses indicate two groups of people we should share Jesus' message with—can you tell who they are?

_____

_____

_____

_____

_____

In addition to helping someone for all eternity by sharing the gospel with them, we are helped, too. Read Philemon verse 6. How do you figure that we gain a better understanding of Christ by sharing our faith?

_____

_____

_____

_____

_____

ACTION

The second inspection asked which you are stronger at, showing or telling people about Jesus. How can you "beef up" the other component in your life? Make a specific plan using this statement, "When I am faced with _____, I will _____."

_____

_____

_____

_____

Write down your Scripture memory verse below.

MEMORY VERSE

NOTES

NOTES

NOTES

COURAGE IS WHAT IT TAKES to stand up and speak; courage is also what it takes to sit down and listen.

Winston Churchill

COURAGE COMES IN ALL KINDS OF FORMS.

Admitting you're wrong. Sharing your faith. Listening to the advice of someone wiser. It takes courage to do God's thing.

Remember the graffiti banner you covered with the fears, challenges, and pressures that Christian teenagers face? Later you tore off a piece, crumpled it up, and laid it at the foot of the cross. **IT ALL COMES BACK TO THE CROSS.**

JESUS BECAME THE ULTIMATE EXAMPLE of

courage when He allowed Himself to be nailed to a tree. Because of the blood He shed, we have a red badge of courage permanently sewn to our souls.

HE'S PUT HIS MARK GUARANTEEING ETERNITY ON US; WHAT DO WE HAVE TO BE AFRAID OF?

TEST OF COURAGE

JOSEPH OF ARIMATHEA, a prominent member of the Council, who was himself waiting for the kingdom of God, went boldly to Pilate and asked for Jesus' body.... Summoning the centurion, he asked him if Jesus had already died. When he learned from the centurion that it was so, he gave the body to Joseph. So Joseph bought some linen cloth, took down the body, wrapped it in the linen, and placed it in a tomb cut out of rock. Then he rolled a stone against the entrance of the tomb.

Mark 15:43–46

YOU HEARD ABOUT A COUPLE of portraits of courage: Roy Pontoh, who was stabbed to death for refusing to renounce his faith, and Julie Moore, who led a Bible study club despite her classmates' mockery and opposition. Your leader mentioned that for many of us, if someone said, "Renounce Jesus or I'll kill you," the choice to be courageous would be obvious. Then you talked about how in America, where we can worship how and who we want, the situations calling for courage can be a lot more subtle.

Big courage or little courage. Dramatic or plain. The distinction is not what matters. What matters is, in that moment, standing firm.

INSPECTION

How do you define courage?

_____

_____

How would you define a courageous Christian?

_____

_____

ANALYSIS

Reread about Joseph of Arimathea (not Mary's husband, a different Joseph) at the top of the previous page.

Joseph was part of the council that handed Jesus over to be put on trial (Mark 15:1). His buddies openly hated Jesus. When Joseph asked for Jesus' body, he wasn't just going against the grain; he was distancing himself from his friends. At that point, his only friend was a dead guy Joseph had no idea was going to rise again in three days. What do you think Joseph would say if you asked him if the social scar was worth it?

_____

_____

_____

_____

The atmosphere in Jerusalem was violent. The crowds gathered into an angry mob and demanded Pilate kill Jesus (Luke 23:18–25). His closest friends were still hiding out, and even while the crowds' voices were still hoarse from shouting "Crucify him!", Joseph is the first to step out and show his devotion to Jesus. What can Joseph teach us about courage?

_____

_____

_____

_____

ACTION

What are some barriers that stop you from being courageous?

_____

_____

W6-D1

What are some situations where you experience these barriers?

_____

_____

_____

_____

During this week memorize the following passage:

BE STRONG AND COURAGEOUS. Do not be afraid or terrified because of them, for the LORD your God goes with you; he will never leave you nor forsake you.

Deuteronomy 31:6

Use the space below to write out the verse or draw a picture that represents it.

MEMORY VERSE

TOOLS OF THE TRADE

THEY WERE ALL TRYING TO FRIGHTEN US, thinking, "Their hands will get too weak for the work, and it will not be completed."

But I prayed, "Now strengthen my hands."

Nehemiah 6:9

YOU LEARNED ABOUT FOUR TOOLS we can use to fight the "fear factor" and find courage. They are prayer, time spent with Jesus, the Holy Spirit, and the knowledge that God is powerful. The next four days we'll examine these tools of the trade one at a time, starting with prayer.

Remember when you were little, and just telling someone about your bad dream made you feel better? Hopefully, high school isn't a nightmare, but God knows it isn't easy to just get through the day sometimes. And on top of that, you're expected to live a bold, Christian example! That takes courage and it's hard when you're feeling weak.

INSPECTION

Have you tried praying when you need strength and courage?

_____

_____

_____

_____

_____

_____

If so, do you feel like it helps? How can you tell?

_____

_____

_____

_____

_____

_____

ANALYSIS

READ PSALM 64. How does the prayer start off? How does it end?

_____

_____

_____

_____

_____

_____

Read through some more of the Psalms. How many more Psalms is it before you get to another one in which David is praying for help and courage? Since David was "a man after God's own heart," how do you think God feels about prayer asking for His help?

_____

_____

_____

_____

_____

_____

ACTION

Reword our Scripture memory verse for the week,
Deuteronomy 31:6, and figure out a way to turn it into a prayer.
Write it down below. Then pray it aloud.

_____

_____

_____

_____

_____

_____

_____

_____

_____

_____

SAVOR THE SAVIOR

WHEN THEY SAW THE COURAGE of Peter and John and realized that they were unschooled, ordinary men, they were astonished and they took note that these men had been with Jesus.

Acts 4:13

DURING THE SIXTH SESSION of *Dig In,* someone read the verse above to the group. You learned that spending time with Jesus makes all the difference. Peter and John were courageous because they had been with Jesus, seeing how He acted with people, how He cured their broken bodies and broken hearts, how He gave His life, and how He defeated death and rose from the grave. Because of the Bible, we can know Jesus, too.

INSPECTION

Why is reading the Bible considered spending time with Him?

_____

_____

_____

_____

_____

_____

_____

What do you notice about your relationship with Jesus (and your openness with others about that relationship) when you are active in your Bible reading? Is there any difference?

_____

_____

_____

_____

ANALYSIS

Whether or not a person acts with courage sometimes depends on how well they know what pleases God. Read 2 Timothy 3:16—4:4. What happens to the person who turns away from the Word?

_____

_____

_____

_____

_____

_____

In light of the passage you just read, what can be gained from memorizing the Bible verses you've been working on?

_____

_____

_____

_____

_____

_____

W6-D3 ACTION

Here's a little homework. Mark is the shortest and fastest-paced of the four Gospels that tell about Jesus' life. Take some time each day to read a bit of it. As you work your way through, notice which stories speak to you most, that are the most revealing about who Jesus is. On a piece of paper or down below, write down the verse numbers of the stories you like.

_____

_____

_____

_____

When you're finished with Mark, look at your list and pick one story to reread and then "retell" to a friend, maybe even a friend who's not a Christian. Stories about Jesus are relevant to our lives; they don't just belong in Sunday school!

IN GOOD COMPANY

"WHENEVER YOU ARE ARRESTED and brought to trial, do not worry beforehand about what to say. Just say whatever is given you at the time, for it is not you speaking, but the Holy Spirit."

Mark 13:11

A FEW WEEKS AGO, we talked about how you're not a lonely soldier but part of the great, big army of God. While you're not surrounded with your comrades as you face every situation, you're still not alone. The Holy Spirit—God's presence!—is inside of you.

INSPECTION

Before Jesus came (like in the Old Testament), the Holy Spirit existed, but He lived outside of people. Why can He live inside of you now?

_____

_____

_____

_____

_____

_____

How do you know He's there?

_____

_____

_____

_____

_____

W6-D4 ANALYSIS

In Acts 9:10–18, what does God give Ananias the power and the courage to do? (Remember that Ananias is a Christian, and Saul kills Christians.) What effect do you think his action had on the spreading of the Gospel? (Read on in Acts if you're not familiar with Saul's story.)

_____

_____

_____

_____

_____

READ ROMANS 8, VERSES 9, 11 AND 26. Who is calling the shots and doing the work? How might this influence your courage and confidence?

_____

_____

_____

_____

_____

ACTION

If you were able to act courageously—with the Holy Spirit as your guide—what effect do you think you could have on those around you?

_____

_____

Spend some time in prayer by asking the Holy Spirit if there is anyone like Saul in your life who He wants to call to Himself.

Then, claiming the promises in our Scripture memory verse and in the verse at the beginning of this day's Bible study, tell God that you're willing to step out of your comfort zone on His behalf! Ask for His presence and His words to help you talk to that person when the time comes.

THE POWERHOUSE

IN HIS RIGHT HAND HE held seven stars, and out of his mouth came a sharp double-edged sword. His face was like the sun shining in all its brilliance. When I saw him, I fell at his feet as though dead. Then he placed his right hand on me and said: "Do not be afraid. I am the First and the Last."

Revelation 1:16–17

THE FOURTH WAY WE CAN find courage is to simply remember that God is a powerhouse! Your leader had volunteers read Psalm 27:1–3, Isaiah 41:10, and Isaiah 43:1–5. Let me remind you what your leader said about these verses:

> God the galaxy-crafter, planet-spinner, and lightning bolt-maker *is with you* as you step into tough situations. He is present with you, at your side, to strengthen you and encourage you. We have no need to give into fears when we know that God is with us.

INSPECTION

What makes God a powerhouse?

_____

_____

_____

_____

_____

_____

_____

How does *His* power give *you* power?

ANALYSIS

Read a great battle story, Judges 7:1–21. Why, if the Midianites had *so* many people, would God tell Gideon to reduce his army? What does it say about God's power?

_____

_____

_____

_____

_____

How did Gideon display courage?

_____

_____

_____

_____

ACTION

In your Training Manual, you wrote about a time when you let fear, social pressure, or other things hold you back from doing what God might have wanted you to do. Using some of the tools we talked about this week, how could you handle a situation like this in the future?

_____

_____

_____

As best as you can, write out your memory verse below, including the Scripture reference.

_____

_____

_____

_____

_____

_____

_____

_____

_____

_____

_____

_____

PRAY THE VERSE. Personalize it and tell God your fears. Ask for courage. Accept His strength.

NOTES

NOTES

> **THE ULTIMATE MEASURE OF A MAN is** not where he stands in moments of comfort and convenience, but where he stands at times of challenge and controversy.
>
> Martin Luther King, Jr.

DURING THE LAST SESSION OF *Dig In,* you and your group discussed the parable about the four soils. You talked about how each soil might look in a teenager's life. It might have been a familiar Scripture passage for you—maybe you've heard multiple sermons on it—but let's look at it in a new light. Rather than seeing the first three soils as lost causes, let's look at each one with hope. Because even if you're the fourth soil, a turn of weather can change rich silt into sand.

SO LET'S TALK ABOUT HOW TO TAKE each soil and submit it to God's tilling hand. Because as we learned, God does not allow you to be tested beyond what you can bear. Translation: each soil has a chance when He is in the picture.

Has some of your seed been snatched up by birds? There is at least one kernel left God can work with.

Did your seed fall on a rocky place? There is rich soil under its surface.

Is your seed among thorns? God can strengthen the smallest sprout.

Did your seed fall on good soil? Wonderful! Fertilize the soil and keep growing!

LET'S GET STARTED!

"A FARMER WENT OUT to sow his seed. As he was scattering the seed, some fell along the path, and the birds came and ate it up."

"When anyone hears the message about the kingdom and does not understand it, the evil one comes and snatches away what was sown in his heart. This is the seed sown along the path."

Matthew 13:3b–4, 19

IN YOUR TRAINING MANUAL, YOU took some time to think about what a scenario might be where a teenager's response to faith is like seed snatched up by birds. Maybe you pictured those birds as peer-pressuring friends or even a person's family. Jesus says whoever would want to snatch away sown seed is on the side of evil, not on the side of God. So be on the lookout!

But there's more to the verse than just the birds. Let's take some time to consider the first part of the interpretation Jesus gave in the verse above: not understanding the message about the Kingdom.

INSPECTION

What do you think "the message about the kingdom" is?

_____

_____

_____

_____

How does not understanding the message about the Kingdom leave a person vulnerable to the birds?

_____

_____

ANALYSIS

Look up verse 12, which is smack in the middle of the four soils passage in Matthew 13. This verse says that people who receive understanding and activate it into their lives will get even more understanding. But those who don't put what's been revealed to them into practice will lose what little understanding they had in the first place. Why do you think God set up this relationship between obedience and understanding? What does it tell you about how you can get more understanding?

_____

_____

Read Job 32:8. Where can we get understanding if we lack it?

_____

_____

What does Proverbs 13:20 say about how the people you hang with will have an effect on your understanding (wisdom)?

_____

_____

ACTION

Your leader talked about soil fertilizers. For the next couple of days, take a minute to examine how you can use each fertilizer on each soil.

So for today, how can you use (fill in a category from below)_____
to fertilize your soil so that you can have understanding about the message of the Kingdom?

Spending time in God's Word
Prayer
Christian friendships
Corporate worship (church)

Work on memorizing the verse below with its reference.

I HAVE HIDDEN YOUR WORD in my heart that I may not sin against you.

Psalm 119:11

Though your seven-week *Over the Edge* journey is almost finished, keep these memory verses fresh! You may even want to crack open the cover from time to time to refresh your memory and your heart!

MEMORY VERSE

"SOME FELL ON ROCKY PLACES, where it did not have much soil. It sprang up quickly, because the soil was shallow. But when the sun came up, the plants were scorched, and they withered because they had no root."

"The one who received the seed that fell on rocky places is the man who hears the word and at once receives it with joy. But since he has no root, he lasts only a short time. When trouble or persecution comes because of the word, he quickly falls away."

Matthew 13:5–6, 20–21

THIS GROUP OF VERSES is the very reason you're holding this journal in your hands. One spiritual high isn't enough *umph!* to spin your propellers for the rest of your life. It takes daily devotion to establish roots, especially in the rocky world we live in. So let's talk rocks.

INSPECTION

What makes your path rocky? What situations or persecutions make it challenging for you to stay close to Jesus?

_____

_____

_____

How can being devoted to God on daily basis help you push your roots through the rocky soil?

_____

_____

_____

W7-D2 ANALYSIS

Rocks that can trip you up and cause you to take your eyes off God can be from outside yourself—like persecution. What does 1 Peter 5:9 say can be encouraging to us as we face external persecution? Will you just keep facing persecution till you're weak in the knees? (Read on to 1 Peter 5:10.)

_____

_____

_____

_____

Some rocks in our path can be internal struggles—like doubt or depression, or just sad circumstances in our lives. Psalm 34:17–18 paints a tender picture about how God responds to the brokenhearted. But look closely at the beginning of verse 17; what do you have to do?

_____

_____

_____

_____

_____

ACTION

Like yesterday, how can you use (fill in a category from the next page)_____
as fertilizer so that you can push your roots past the rocky topsoil?_____

_____

_____

Spending time in God's Word
Prayer
Christian friendships
Corporate worship (church)

If you're struggling or feeling broken, cry out to God right now. Lay it all out for Him and give Him the chance to come close and give you strength and hope.

_____

_____

_____

_____

_____

"OTHER SEED FELL AMONG THORNS, which grew up and choked the plants."

"The one who received the seed that fell among the thorns is the man who hears the word, but the worries of this life and the deceitfulness of wealth choke it, making it unfruitful."

Matthew 13:7, 22

REMEMBER THE STORY YOU HEARD about Peter and Jesus walking on the water? Peter stepped out in faith, but the raging waves and howling winds took his attention and down, down, down he sank—until Jesus got a hold of him again. That's like this part of the parable. The world around us can be swirling, but if we keep our eyes on Jesus, we can have the peace and certainty in our hearts to keep stepping forward.

INSPECTION

What is fundamentally wrong with worrying?

_____

_____

_____

_____

What is deceitful about wealth?

_____

_____

_____

_____

ANALYSIS

READ MATTHEW 6:19–34. What do these passages teach us about…

… *Worry*

_____

_____

_____

But we do worry. What should we do about it? (See 1 Peter 5:7).

_____

_____

_____

… *Money*

_____

_____

_____

Luke 12:16–21 tells the parable of the rich fool. What does it mean to be rich toward God?

_____

_____

_____

_____

Measure your "richness toward God." How does it look?

_____

_____

_____

W7-D3 ACTION

How can you use (fill in a category from below)

_____

as fertilizer so that you don't get choked by the worries and wealth of this life?

_____

_____

_____

_____

_____

_____

Spending time in God's Word
Prayer
Christian friendships
Corporate worship (church)

HOPE IN THE GOOD SOIL

"STILL OTHER SEED FELL on good soil, where it produced a crop—a hundred, sixty or thirty times what was sown."

"But the one who received the seed that fell on good soil is the man who hears the word and understands it. He produces a crop, yielding a hundred, sixty or thirty times what was sown."

Matthew 13:8, 23

THINK IT'S SMOOTH SAILING if your seed has fallen on good soil? Apart from the guarantee Jesus gave us in John 16:33 that "in this world you will have trouble," just staying faithful in your day-to-day life can be challenging. An example from your *Dig In* experience is the story you heard about Polycarp. He was martyred in his old age, but remember what your leader focused on? How Polycarp had remained faithful for 86 years. Faith isn't always full of dramatic moments; sometimes it's the daily plunking along when God is paying the most attention.

INSPECTION

What does it mean to produce a crop like in the verse above?

_____

_____

_____

_____

_____

_____

What kind of crop are you producing?

_____
_____
_____
_____
_____

ANALYSIS

Read the stories of another couple of "old" saints in Luke chapter 2: Simeon, Luke 2:25–35, and Anna, Luke 2:36–38. Other than Joseph and Mary, these were the first people who could see that Jesus—even as a helpless baby—was the promised Messiah. Why do you suppose that was? What was so special about them?

_____
_____
_____
_____
_____
_____

Good soil needs enduring care and attention. But an enduring faith can only be a response; we don't have it in us on our own. Slowly read Psalm 136. What can prompt endurance in us?

_____
_____
_____
_____
_____
_____
_____

ACTION

How can you use (fill in a category from below)

_____

as fertilizer to keep your soil rich and productive?

_____

_____

_____

_____

_____

_____

_____

Spending time in God's Word
Prayer
Christian friendships
Corporate worship (church)

ENCOURAGEMENT

AFTER PAUL AND SILAS came out of the prison, they went to Lydia's house, where they met with the brothers and encouraged them. Then they left.

Acts 16:40

HOW DID YOU FEEL AFTER YOU READ THE

sign that your *Dig In* friends filled with encouragement and compliments about you? You probably didn't glance at it once and throw it in the trash. If you're like most people, you reread it a few times, let the words soak into your skin. Refreshing wasn't it?

This week you've seen that even during rocky spots in your faith, there is hope for recovery! And the friend, the acquaintance, even the stranger you meet will have some rocky spots, too. Inviting Christ into those tough times is up to the individual, but the encouragement you can give (and receive!) can make all the difference.

INSPECTION

How often do you make a habit of encouraging those around you?

_____

_____

_____

_____

_____

If not, what is holding you back? If you keep a
kind word to yourself and don't share it, who is
pleased—God or Satan?

W7-D5

ANALYSIS

In the verse above, what appears to be the sole purpose of Paul
and Silas's visit?

READ ROMANS 15:1-7. In verses 4 and 5, where are we
told we can find encouragement? What two things are accomplished by our encouraging each other (see verses 6 and 7)?

ACTION

Below, write out your Scripture memory verse with its
reference.

W7-D5

Flip back through the other six "Action" segments of your journal. How are you doing with some of the goals and challenges presented to you? Take a moment to write down some successes and note the areas that could still use some work. Praise God for His work in you and ask His blessing and empowerment as you live out all you've learned.

_____

_____

_____

_____

CONGRATULATIONS ON COMPLETING YOUR JOURNAL! GOOD JOB!!

NOTES

NOTES

NOTES